# BASICS OF TOKENOMICS

PART OF OUR SERIES:

# TOMORROW'S TECH: UNDERSTANDING THE BASICS

# LIMITLESS PUBLISHING @ 2024

# Table of Contents

## Chapter 1: Introduction to Tokenomics .................. 1
- Definition of Tokenomics .................. 1
- Importance of Tokenomics in the context of Blockchain Technology .................. 2
- Brief history and evolution of tokenomics .................. 4
- Key concepts and terminologies related to tokenomics .................. 6

## Chapter 2: Types of Tokens .................. 8
- Overview of different types of tokens (security tokens, utility tokens, payment tokens, etc.) .................. 8
- Characteristics and use cases of each type of token .................. 10
- Regulatory considerations for different types of tokens .................. 12
- Token standards (ERC-20, ERC-721, etc.) and their significance .................. 13

## Chapter 3: Token Issuance and Distribution .................. 16
- Process of token creation and issuance .................. 16
- Token distribution methods (ICO, IEO, STO, airdrops, etc.) .................. 17
- Factors to consider when deciding on the token distribution model .................. 19
- Token supply dynamics and inflation mechanisms .................. 21

## Chapter 4: Tokenomics Design and Analysis .................. 23
- Designing a token economy model .................. 23
- Balancing token utility and scarcity .................. 24
- Token velocity and its impact on the ecosystem .................. 26
- Tools and methodologies for analyzing tokenomics models .................. 28

## Chapter 5: Token Valuation and Metrics .................. 30
- Valuation methods for tokens .................. 30
- Key metrics to evaluate the health and performance of a token economy .................. 31
- Token price dynamics and factors influencing token value .................. 33
- Case studies of successful token projects and their valuation strategies .................. 35

## Chapter 6: Future Trends and Challenges in Tokenomics .................. 37
- Emerging trends in the field of tokenomics .................. 37
- Challenges and limitations of existing tokenomics models .................. 39
- Potential regulatory developments and their implications on token economies .................. 41
- Predictions for the future of tokenomics and its role in the broader financial ecosystem 42

# Chapter 1: Introduction to Tokenomics

## - Definition of Tokenomics

Tokenomics, short for token economics, refers to the study and analysis of the economics behind token-based systems. It involves understanding how tokens function within a particular ecosystem, including their creation, distribution, and utilization. Tokenomics is a crucial concept in the world of blockchain technology and cryptocurrency, as tokens play a fundamental role in various decentralized platforms and applications.

At its core, tokenomics aims to design and implement token systems that align incentives among participants to achieve specific objectives. These objectives can vary widely depending on the context, such as raising funds through token sales (Initial Coin Offerings), incentivizing user participation in a decentralized network, or creating mechanisms for governance and decision-making within a community.

One key aspect of tokenomics is token utility, which refers to the practical uses and functions of a token within its ecosystem. Tokens can serve various purposes, such as providing access to services, representing ownership rights, facilitating transactions, or participating in governance processes. The design of tokenomics involves determining how tokens are distributed, how they are used, and how their value is maintained over time.

Another important consideration in tokenomics is token supply and demand dynamics. The total supply of tokens, their rate of issuance, and factors influencing demand all play a significant role in determining the value of a token. Economic principles such as scarcity, utility, and network effects come into play when analyzing tokenomics and predicting the behavior of token markets.

Tokenomics also encompasses mechanisms for ensuring the sustainability and security of token ecosystems. This includes designing token distribution models that incentivize long-term participation and discourage manipulative behavior. Additionally, tokenomics involves implementing mechanisms for preventing fraud, ensuring transparency, and fostering trust among participants.

In summary, tokenomics is a multidisciplinary field that combines elements of economics, game theory, computer science, and cryptography. By understanding the fundamentals of tokenomics, stakeholders can make informed decisions about participating in token-based systems, designing new tokens, and analyzing the economic implications of blockchain projects.

## - Importance of Tokenomics in the context of Blockchain Technology

Tokenomics, a portmanteau of "token" and "economics," refers to the economics of tokens or digital assets within a blockchain ecosystem. Tokenomics plays a crucial role in the context of blockchain technology for several reasons:

1. Incentive Mechanisms: Tokenomics helps design incentive mechanisms within blockchain networks. By creating tokens that are essential for accessing or utilizing the network, developers can encourage desired behaviors such as network participation, content creation, or governance involvement.

2. Network Governance: Tokens can be used to facilitate decentralized governance within blockchain projects. Token holders often have voting rights proportional to their holdings, allowing them to participate in decision-making processes related to protocol upgrades, fund allocation, and other key governance issues.

3. Value Capture: Tokenomics enables value capture within blockchain ecosystems. Tokens can represent ownership of a particular asset, access to a service, or a share of network revenue. This allows participants to capture value from the growth of the network and incentivizes them to contribute to its development.

4. Monetary Policy: Tokenomics involves designing the monetary policy of a blockchain system, including aspects such as token distribution, inflation rate, and supply cap. A well-designed tokenomics model can help maintain price stability, prevent inflation, and ensure the long-term sustainability of the network.

5. Security and Anti-Sybil Measures: Tokens can be used to enhance security and prevent sybil attacks within blockchain networks. By requiring participants to hold a certain amount of tokens as collateral or staking them to validate transactions, tokenomics can deter malicious actors and ensure the integrity of the network.

6. Interoperability and Standardization: Tokenomics can promote interoperability and standardization across different blockchain platforms. By establishing common token standards and economic models, tokenomics can facilitate seamless interaction between disparate networks and foster the growth of the overall blockchain ecosystem.

7. Market Dynamics: Tokenomics influences market dynamics within blockchain ecosystems. Factors such as token supply, demand, liquidity, and distribution can impact token prices, trading volume, and overall market sentiment, making tokenomics a crucial consideration for investors and traders.

In conclusion, tokenomics plays a fundamental role in shaping the economic and governance structures of blockchain technology. By designing robust tokenomics models, blockchain projects can incentivize participation, foster decentralization, capture value, and ensure the long-term sustainability and growth of their networks. Understanding the importance of tokenomics is essential for anyone looking to engage with blockchain technology and its associated ecosystems.

## - Brief history and evolution of tokenomics

Tokenomics, a term derived from the words "token" and "economics," refers to the study of the economics, design, and creation of tokens within a blockchain ecosystem. Tokens are digital assets that can represent various things such as utility, ownership, or access rights within a decentralized network. The concept of tokenomics has evolved significantly since the inception of blockchain technology.

**Early Days of Tokenomics:**
The early days of tokenomics can be traced back to the introduction of Bitcoin in 2009 by the pseudonymous creator, Satoshi Nakamoto. Bitcoin, the first decentralized cryptocurrency, introduced the concept of using digital tokens as a medium of exchange without the need for intermediaries such as banks. The success of Bitcoin paved the way for the development of other cryptocurrencies and tokens.

**Ethereum and Smart Contracts:**
In 2015, Ethereum, a blockchain platform, was launched, introducing the concept of smart contracts. Smart contracts are self-executing contracts with the terms of the agreement directly written into code. Ethereum enabled the creation of custom tokens through its ERC-20 token standard, allowing developers to issue their own tokens on the Ethereum blockchain. This marked a significant milestone in the evolution of tokenomics, as it facilitated the creation of a wide variety of tokens for various purposes.

**Tokenization of Assets:**
As blockchain technology continued to mature, the concept of tokenizing real-world assets emerged. Tokenization involves representing physical assets, such as real estate, art, or commodities, as digital tokens on a blockchain. Tokenization has the potential to increase liquidity, reduce transaction costs, and enable fractional ownership of assets that were previously illiquid. This application of tokenomics has gained traction in various industries, including real estate, finance, and supply chain management.

**DeFi and Governance Tokens:**
The rise of decentralized finance (DeFi) has further expanded the scope of tokenomics. DeFi protocols enable various financial services, such as lending, borrowing, and trading, without the need for traditional intermediaries. Governance tokens are a type of token that grants holders voting rights to participate in the decision-making process of a decentralized protocol. Governance tokens have become an essential component of many DeFi projects, shaping the future direction of these platforms.

**Future Trends and Innovations:**
Looking ahead, the field of tokenomics is likely to continue evolving with new innovations and applications. Non-fungible tokens (NFTs), unique digital assets that represent ownership of a specific item or piece of content, have gained widespread popularity in recent years. Additionally, advancements in blockchain scalability, interoperability, and privacy solutions are expected to further enhance the capabilities of tokenomics.

In conclusion, the history and evolution of tokenomics demonstrate the transformative potential of blockchain technology in redefining traditional economic systems. As the ecosystem continues to grow and mature, tokenomics is poised to play a central role in shaping the future of decentralized finance, asset tokenization, and digital ownership.

**- Key concepts and terminologies related to tokenomics**

Tokenomics is a field that combines principles of economics, game theory, and computer science to analyze and design the economic structures of blockchain-based systems. Understanding key concepts and terminologies related to tokenomics is essential for anyone looking to navigate the complex world of digital assets and decentralized protocols. Below are some important terms to know:

1. Token: A token is a digital asset that represents a unit of value on a blockchain. Tokens can have various functions within a blockchain ecosystem, such as utility tokens used for accessing services or security tokens representing ownership of assets.

2. Cryptoeconomics: Cryptoeconomics is the study of the economic incentives and mechanisms underlying blockchain protocols. It involves designing systems that use cryptographic techniques to create economic incentives for participants to behave in certain ways.

3. Token Utility: Token utility refers to the usefulness or value that a token provides within a specific ecosystem. Tokens may have utility for accessing services, participating in governance, or receiving rewards.

4. Token Supply: Token supply refers to the total number of tokens that exist within a blockchain ecosystem. The token supply can be fixed, inflationary, or deflationary, depending on the design of the tokenomics.

5. Token Distribution: Token distribution refers to how tokens are allocated and distributed within a blockchain ecosystem. Fair and transparent token distribution is crucial for ensuring the long-term success and decentralization of

a project.

6. Tokenomics Model: A tokenomics model outlines the economic design of a blockchain project, including token distribution, token utility, governance mechanisms, and incentives for participants. A well-designed tokenomics model is essential for achieving the project's goals and sustainability.

7. Token Sale: A token sale, also known as an initial coin offering (ICO) or token generation event (TGE), is a fundraising method used by blockchain projects to distribute tokens to investors in exchange for funding. Token sales play a crucial role in bootstrapping new projects and building communities around them.

8. Governance Token: Governance tokens are tokens that grant holders the right to participate in the decision-making processes of a blockchain protocol. Holders of governance tokens can vote on proposals, such as protocol upgrades or changes to tokenomics.

9. Decentralized Finance (DeFi): DeFi refers to a set of financial applications and services built on blockchain technology that aims to replace traditional financial intermediaries with smart contracts. DeFi projects often have their own tokenomics models and governance structures.

10. Token Burn: Token burn is a mechanism used to reduce the total supply of tokens by permanently removing them from circulation. Token burns can be used to create scarcity, increase the value of remaining tokens, and align incentives for token holders.

By familiarizing yourself with these key concepts and terminologies related to tokenomics, you will be better equipped to navigate the rapidly evolving world of blockchain technology and digital assets.

# Chapter 2: Types of Tokens

**- Overview of different types of tokens (security tokens, utility tokens, payment tokens, etc.)**

Tokens are a fundamental component of the cryptocurrency and blockchain ecosystem, each serving a specific purpose and function within their respective projects. Understanding the various types of tokens is essential for investors, developers, and enthusiasts alike. Here, we explore the main categories of tokens:

## Security Tokens

Security tokens represent ownership of an asset, similar to traditional securities like stocks or bonds. These tokens are subject to regulations from financial authorities and are designed to provide legal rights to the holders. Security tokens often offer dividends, profit shares, or voting rights within the issuing company. Due to their regulatory nature, security tokens require compliance with securities laws, making them a more restricted asset class.

## Utility Tokens

Utility tokens are designed to provide users with access to a product or service within a specific platform or ecosystem. These tokens are not considered investments, but rather function as a form of payment for utilizing the features of the associated project. Utility tokens are commonly used in decentralized applications (DApps) and blockchain networks to incentivize users and facilitate transactions within the ecosystem.

## Payment Tokens

Payment tokens, also known as cryptocurrencies, are digital assets used for conducting transactions and transferring value between parties. These tokens serve as a medium of exchange and store of value within the blockchain network. Popular examples of payment tokens include Bitcoin (BTC) and Litecoin (LTC). Payment tokens are decentralized and operate independently of traditional financial systems, offering users greater control over their funds and transactions.

## Governance Tokens

Governance tokens are used to participate in the decision-making processes of a decentralized protocol or platform. Holders of governance tokens have voting rights on proposals, upgrades, and changes to the network's parameters. These tokens empower users to shape the future development and direction of the project, fostering a more democratic and community-driven ecosystem. Governance tokens are crucial for decentralized autonomous organizations (DAOs) and governance structures in blockchain projects.

## Non-Fungible Tokens (NFTs)

Non-fungible tokens (NFTs) represent unique digital assets that are indivisible and cannot be exchanged on a one-to-one basis. Each NFT has distinct properties and ownership, making them ideal for representing digital art, collectibles, and in-game assets. NFTs are recorded on the blockchain, providing provenance, authenticity, and scarcity to digital items. The rise of NFTs has revolutionized the concept of ownership in the digital realm, opening up new opportunities for creators and collectors.

In conclusion, the diverse range of token types plays a vital role in shaping the cryptocurrency and blockchain landscape. Understanding the unique characteristics and functions of each token category is essential for navigating the evolving tokenomics space and leveraging the full potential of blockchain technology.

---

This section provides a comprehensive overview of the main types of tokens discussed in the book 'Basics of Tokenomics'.

## - Characteristics and use cases of each type of token

Tokens are digital assets that represent a variety of assets or utilities on a blockchain network. There are several types of tokens, each with its own unique characteristics and use cases. In this section, we will explore the different types of tokens and their applications.

1. Utility Tokens:
Utility tokens are the most common type of tokens and are designed to provide access to a specific product or service within a blockchain ecosystem. These tokens are not considered as investments but rather as tools that enable users to interact with the platform. Utility tokens can be used for accessing features, paying for services, or participating in governance decisions within the network. Examples of utility tokens include Binance Coin (BNB) and Ethereum (ETH), which are used to pay for transaction fees on their respective platforms.

2. Security Tokens:
Security tokens represent ownership of a tradable asset, such as equity, debt, or real estate. These tokens are subject to regulatory requirements and are considered as investments. Security tokens offer investors ownership rights, profit-sharing, and voting privileges. They are often issued through Security Token Offerings (STOs) and provide a way to tokenize traditional assets, making them more liquid and accessible. Security tokens must comply with securities regulations to ensure investor protection.

3. Payment Tokens:
Payment tokens, also known as cryptocurrencies, are designed to be used as a medium of exchange for goods and services. These tokens facilitate transactions on blockchain networks and enable users to transfer value across borders quickly and securely. Payment tokens are decentralized, meaning they operate independently of traditional financial institutions. Examples of payment tokens include Bitcoin (BTC) and Litecoin (LTC), which can be used for online purchases, remittances, and investments.

4. Governance Tokens:
Governance tokens give holders the right to participate in decision-making processes within a decentralized network. These tokens are used to vote on protocol upgrades, funding proposals, and other governance-related matters. Governance tokens incentivize community involvement and empower token holders to shape the future of the platform. Examples of governance tokens include Compound (COMP) and Maker (MKR), which allow users to vote on changes to their respective protocols and manage decentralized finance (DeFi) platforms.

5. Non-Fungible Tokens (NFTs):
Non-Fungible Tokens (NFTs) are unique digital assets that represent ownership of a specific item, such as artwork, collectibles, or virtual real estate. NFTs are indivisible and cannot be exchanged on a one-to-one basis like cryptocurrencies. Each NFT has a distinct value and can be bought, sold, and traded on NFT marketplaces. These tokens are often used in digital art, gaming, and intellectual property rights. Examples of NFTs include CryptoKitties, NBA Top Shot moments, and digital art pieces sold as NFTs.

In conclusion, tokens play a crucial role in the blockchain ecosystem by enabling various functionalities and use cases. Understanding the characteristics and applications of each type of token is essential for navigating the rapidly evolving world of tokenomics and decentralized finance.

## - Regulatory considerations for different types of tokens

Regulatory considerations play a crucial role in shaping the tokenomics of various digital assets. Depending on the type of token issued, different regulations may apply. In this section, we will explore the regulatory considerations for different types of tokens as outlined in the book 'Basics of Tokenomics'.

1. Security Tokens:

Security tokens represent ownership of an underlying asset, such as equity in a company, real estate, or debt instruments. These tokens are considered securities by regulatory bodies in many jurisdictions, including the SEC in the United States. Issuers of security tokens must comply with securities laws, which may include registration requirements, disclosure obligations, and restrictions on who can invest in these tokens. It is essential for issuers to carefully navigate these regulations to ensure compliance and avoid legal repercussions.

2. Utility Tokens:

Utility tokens are designed to provide access to a product or service within a specific ecosystem. These tokens do not represent ownership of any underlying asset and are not considered securities in many jurisdictions. However, regulatory bodies are increasingly scrutinizing utility tokens to ensure they do not fall under the definition of securities. Issuers should clearly articulate the utility of their tokens and avoid making any promises of future profits to maintain compliance with regulations.

3. Payment Tokens:

Payment tokens, such as Bitcoin and other cryptocurrencies, are used primarily as a medium of exchange. These tokens are not considered securities in most cases but may still be subject to regulations related to anti-money laundering (AML) and know your customer (KYC) requirements. Exchanges and businesses dealing with payment tokens must adhere to these regulations to prevent illegal activities, such as money laundering and terrorist financing.

4. Stablecoins:

Stablecoins are digital assets pegged to a stable asset, such as a fiat currency or a commodity, to minimize price volatility. Depending on the structure and backing of stablecoins, they may fall under different regulatory frameworks. For example, stablecoins backed 1:1 by fiat currency may be subject to regulations governing traditional currencies, while algorithmic stablecoins may face scrutiny for potential risks to financial stability.

In conclusion, regulatory considerations for different types of tokens are essential for ensuring compliance with laws and regulations governing the issuance and trading of digital assets. Issuers and market participants must stay informed about evolving regulatory landscapes to navigate the complex web of rules and requirements effectively. Failure to comply with regulations can lead to legal consequences, financial penalties, and reputational damage for token issuers and stakeholders involved in the token economy.

## - Token standards (ERC-20, ERC-721, etc.) and their significance

Token standards play a crucial role in the world of blockchain and cryptocurrency as they define the rules and functionalities of tokens issued on a specific blockchain platform. In this section, we will delve into some of the most popular token standards, such as ERC-20 and ERC-721, and explore their significance in the tokenomics ecosystem.

1. ERC-20 Standard:
ERC-20 stands for Ethereum Request for Comment 20 and is the most widely

adopted token standard on the Ethereum blockchain. ERC-20 tokens are fungible, meaning each token is identical and interchangeable with another token of the same type. This standard defines a set of rules and functions that a token contract must implement in order to be considered ERC-20 compliant.

Significance of ERC-20:
- Interoperability: ERC-20 tokens adhere to a common set of rules, making it easier for different tokens to interact with each other within the Ethereum ecosystem.
- Liquidity: ERC-20 tokens are supported by a wide range of wallets, exchanges, and decentralized applications (dApps), which enhances their liquidity and ease of use.
- Crowdfunding: The ERC-20 standard has been widely used for launching Initial Coin Offerings (ICOs) and token sales, enabling projects to raise funds by issuing tokens on the Ethereum blockchain.

2. ERC-721 Standard:
ERC-721 is a non-fungible token (NFT) standard on the Ethereum blockchain, where each token is unique and not interchangeable with any other token. ERC-721 tokens are used to represent ownership of digital or physical assets, such as collectibles, game items, real estate, and art.

Significance of ERC-721:
- Ownership and Scarcity: ERC-721 tokens enable the creation of unique digital assets with distinct ownership records, allowing for the tokenization of scarce or one-of-a-kind items.
- Digital Collectibles: The ERC-721 standard has revolutionized the concept of digital collectibles, enabling the creation and trading of unique items in the form of NFTs.
- Use Cases: ERC-721 tokens have been used in various industries, including gaming, art, music, and real estate, to tokenize and transfer ownership of assets in a secure and transparent manner.

3. Other Token Standards:
Apart from ERC-20 and ERC-721, there are several other token standards such as ERC-1155, ERC-777, and BEP-20 (for Binance Smart Chain) that cater to specific use cases and functionalities within the blockchain ecosystem.

In conclusion, token standards play a vital role in standardizing token creation, transfer, and management on blockchain platforms. Understanding the significance of token standards like ERC-20 and ERC-721 is essential for developers, businesses, and investors looking to leverage the potential of blockchain technology and tokenomics.

# Chapter 3: Token Issuance and Distribution

## - Process of token creation and issuance

Token creation and issuance are crucial steps in the development and deployment of a token economy. The process involves several key considerations, ranging from technological aspects to regulatory compliance. Below is a detailed section on the process of token creation and issuance:

1. Define Token Purpose: The first step in creating a token is to clearly define its purpose. This involves determining what utility or function the token will serve within the ecosystem. Tokens can represent ownership rights, access to services, voting rights, or other forms of value.

2. Choose Token Standards: There are various token standards, such as ERC-20, ERC-721, and BEP-20, each with its own set of rules and functionalities. The choice of token standard depends on the specific requirements of the project. For example, ERC-20 tokens are widely used for fungible tokens, while ERC-721 tokens are ideal for non-fungible tokens.

3. Token Design: Once the purpose and standards are defined, the next step is to design the token. This involves determining the token supply, decimal places, symbol, and other parameters. Token design should align with the project's goals and be user-friendly for investors and users.

4. Smart Contract Development: Tokens are typically created and managed through smart contracts on blockchain platforms like Ethereum. Smart contract development involves writing code to define the token's behavior, including functions for issuing, transferring, and burning tokens. Security audits are essential to ensure the smart contract is secure and free from vulnerabilities.

5. Token Issuance: After the smart contract is developed and audited, the token issuance process can begin. Tokens can be minted (created) and distributed to investors through a token sale, airdrop, or other distribution methods. Issuance should be transparent, with clear documentation on how the tokens are distributed and managed.

6. Compliance and Legal Considerations: Token creation and issuance must comply with relevant laws and regulations, such as securities laws and anti-money laundering (AML) regulations. It is important to consult legal experts to ensure that the token offering is compliant and does not pose any regulatory risks.

7. Token Distribution: Once the tokens are created and issued, they need to be distributed to investors and users. This can involve listing the tokens on cryptocurrency exchanges, integrating them into wallets and dApps, and implementing marketing strategies to promote token adoption.

8. Tokenomics and Governance: Tokenomics refers to the economic design of the token ecosystem, including factors such as token supply, distribution mechanisms, and incentives. Governance mechanisms should also be established to enable token holders to participate in decision-making processes and ensure the sustainability of the ecosystem.

In conclusion, the process of token creation and issuance is a complex and multifaceted undertaking that requires careful planning, technical expertise, and regulatory compliance. By following best practices and engaging with relevant stakeholders, token projects can create a robust and successful token economy.

- **Token distribution methods (ICO, IEO, STO, airdrops, etc.)**
Token distribution methods play a crucial role in the successful launch and operation of a token-based project. In this section, we will delve into various token distribution methods, including Initial Coin Offerings (ICOs), Initial

Exchange Offerings (IEOs), Security Token Offerings (STOs), airdrops, and more.

1. Initial Coin Offerings (ICOs):
ICOs are one of the most popular methods of distributing tokens to the public. In an ICO, a project issues and sells a new cryptocurrency token to investors in exchange for established cryptocurrencies like Bitcoin or Ethereum. Investors purchase these tokens with the expectation that the project will be successful, and the tokens will increase in value over time.

2. Initial Exchange Offerings (IEOs):
IEOs are similar to ICOs but conducted through cryptocurrency exchanges. In an IEO, a project partners with a crypto exchange to launch the token sale directly on the platform. This provides a level of trust and security for investors since the exchange typically vets the projects before hosting their token sale.

3. Security Token Offerings (STOs):
STOs differ from ICOs in that they offer tokens that represent ownership in real-world assets, such as equity in a company or a share of profits. STOs are subject to securities regulations and provide investors with legal rights and protections. This makes STOs a more regulated and secure option for token distribution, appealing to traditional investors.

4. Airdrops:
Airdrops involve distributing tokens for free to existing cryptocurrency holders or to users who perform certain tasks, such as joining a Telegram group or following the project on social media. Airdrops are often used to increase awareness, build a community, and incentivize user participation in a project.

5. Token Sales and Private Placements:
Token sales can also be conducted through private placements, where tokens are offered to a select group of investors before being made available to the public.

This method allows projects to raise capital from strategic investors or venture capitalists before launching a public token sale.

6. Token Burn and Buyback Programs:
Some projects implement token burn and buyback programs as part of their token distribution strategy. Token burn involves permanently removing a certain number of tokens from circulation, thereby reducing the overall supply and potentially increasing the value of the remaining tokens. Buyback programs involve a project repurchasing its own tokens from the market, usually to redistribute or retire them.

Overall, the choice of token distribution method depends on various factors, including the project's goals, target audience, regulatory considerations, and fundraising requirements. By selecting the most suitable distribution method, projects can effectively engage with investors, build a strong community, and drive the success of their tokenomics model.

## - Factors to consider when deciding on the token distribution model

Deciding on the token distribution model is a crucial aspect of any tokenomics design, as it directly impacts the functionality, value, and overall success of a project. Various factors need to be carefully considered while determining the token distribution model to ensure fairness, sustainability, and alignment with the project's objectives. Below are some key factors that should be taken into account:

1. Project Goals and Objectives: The distribution model should be aligned with the project's goals and objectives. For example, if the project aims to create a decentralized governance system, the distribution model should prioritize decentralization and community participation.

2. Token Utility: Consider how the tokens will be used within the ecosystem. Tokens can serve various purposes such as payment for goods and services, governance rights, staking for network security, or access to specific features. The distribution model should ensure that the tokens are distributed to incentivize desired behaviors and provide value to users.

3. Token Supply: Determine the total token supply and how it will be distributed over time. Factors such as inflation rate, token release schedule, and token emission mechanisms should be carefully considered to maintain a balance between scarcity and utility.

4. Distribution Mechanism: Decide on the method of token distribution, whether it will be through a public sale, private sale, airdrop, liquidity mining, or other mechanisms. Each distribution method has its own advantages and considerations, such as community engagement, investor participation, and regulatory compliance.

5. Token Allocation: Define how the tokens will be allocated among various stakeholders, including founders, team members, advisors, investors, community members, and ecosystem development. Ensure a fair and transparent allocation process to prevent centralization of token ownership and promote long-term sustainability.

6. Vesting Periods: Implement vesting periods for tokens allocated to team members, advisors, and early investors to align their interests with the long-term success of the project. Vesting schedules can help prevent token dumping and ensure commitment to the project's growth.

7. Regulatory Compliance: Consider regulatory requirements and legal implications related to token distribution, especially in the context of securities laws and financial regulations. Compliance with relevant laws is essential to avoid legal risks and ensure the project's legitimacy.

8. Community Engagement: Involve the community in the token distribution process to foster a sense of ownership and participation. Implement mechanisms for community feedback, governance voting, and transparency to build trust and loyalty among token holders.

Conclusion

In conclusion, the token distribution model plays a crucial role in shaping the success and sustainability of a project. By considering factors such as project goals, token utility, supply, distribution mechanism, allocation, vesting periods, regulatory compliance, and community engagement, project teams can design a fair, transparent, and effective token distribution model that aligns with the project's vision and objectives. Careful planning and execution of the token distribution strategy can contribute to the long-term success and adoption of the project within the crypto ecosystem.

- **Token supply dynamics and inflation mechanisms**
Token supply dynamics and inflation mechanisms are crucial components of tokenomics, determining the growth and sustainability of a token ecosystem. In this section, we will explore how token supply dynamics and inflation mechanisms impact the overall value and circulation of tokens within a blockchain network.

**Token Supply Dynamics:**
Token supply dynamics refer to the factors that influence the total supply of tokens available within a blockchain network. The key elements that shape token supply dynamics include:
1. Initial Token Distribution: The way in which tokens are initially distributed among investors, developers, community members, and other stakeholders.
2. Token Minting and Burning: Processes by which new tokens are created

(minting) or removed from circulation (burning) to manage supply and demand dynamics.

3. Token Vesting: Rules governing the gradual release of tokens to recipients over a specified period, often used to incentivize long-term engagement and prevent sudden sell-offs.

4. Token Lock-ups: Mechanisms that restrict the transferability of tokens for a certain period, promoting stability and preventing market manipulation.

**Inflation Mechanisms:**

Inflation mechanisms determine how the token supply changes over time, impacting factors such as scarcity, purchasing power, and network security. Common inflation mechanisms in tokenomics include:

1. Fixed Supply: Tokens with a fixed maximum supply, like Bitcoin, have a deflationary design, as the total supply cannot exceed a predetermined limit. This scarcity can drive up token value over time.

2. Linear Inflation: Tokens with a linear inflation model release a consistent amount of new tokens into circulation over time. This approach aims to balance supply growth with demand to maintain price stability.

3. Proof of Stake (PoS): PoS consensus mechanisms reward token holders with new tokens for participating in network validation and governance, incentivizing stakeholder engagement and network security.

4. Emission Schedules: Token projects often define emission schedules that outline how new tokens are minted and distributed over time, providing transparency and predictability for investors and stakeholders.

Overall, token supply dynamics and inflation mechanisms play a vital role in shaping the economic model of a blockchain network. By carefully designing and implementing these mechanisms, token projects can influence factors such as price stability, network security, and community engagement to create a sustainable and thriving ecosystem for their tokens.

# Chapter 4: Tokenomics Design and Analysis

## - Designing a token economy model

Designing a token economy model is a crucial aspect of creating a successful blockchain project or cryptocurrency. A well-thought-out token economy can incentivize desired behaviors, create network effects, and drive the value of the token. In this section, we will delve into the key considerations and steps involved in designing a token economy model.

1. Define the Purpose and Goals: The first step in designing a token economy model is to clearly define the purpose and goals of the token. Are you creating a utility token for accessing a specific service or platform, a security token for investment purposes, or a governance token for voting rights? Understanding the purpose of the token will guide the design process.

2. Tokenomics Design: Tokenomics refers to the economic model of the token, including its distribution, supply, utility, and value proposition. Key aspects to consider in tokenomics design include:
   - Token Distribution: How will the tokens be distributed initially? Will there be a token sale, airdrops, or mining rewards?
   - Token Supply: What is the total supply of tokens, and will it be fixed or inflationary?
   - Token Utility: How will the token be used within the ecosystem? What benefits or privileges will token holders receive?
   - Token Value Proposition: What factors will drive the value of the token, such as scarcity, utility, or demand?

3. Incentive Mechanisms: A successful token economy model should include incentive mechanisms to encourage user participation and engagement. This can include rewards for staking tokens, providing liquidity, or contributing to the ecosystem in other ways. Designing effective incentive mechanisms can help

create a vibrant and active community around the token.

4. Governance Structure: If the token has governance functions, it is essential to design a governance structure that is transparent, inclusive, and effective. Token holders should have a say in decision-making processes, such as protocol upgrades, fund allocation, or changes to the token economics.

5. Ecosystem Integration: Consider how the token economy model fits within the broader ecosystem. Will the token interact with other tokens or protocols? How will partnerships and collaborations impact the token's value and utility?

6. Security and Compliance: Ensure that the token economy model complies with relevant regulatory requirements and security best practices. Conduct thorough security audits and seek legal advice to mitigate risks and ensure compliance with laws and regulations.

7. Iterative Design and Feedback: Designing a token economy model is an ongoing process that requires feedback and iteration. Monitor the performance of the token economy, gather feedback from users and stakeholders, and be prepared to make adjustments to improve the model over time.

In conclusion, designing a token economy model involves a careful consideration of the token's purpose, tokenomics, incentive mechanisms, governance structure, ecosystem integration, security, and compliance. By following these key considerations and steps, you can create a robust and effective token economy model that drives value and success for your blockchain project.

### - Balancing token utility and scarcity

In the realm of tokenomics, the delicate balance between token utility and scarcity plays a crucial role in determining the value and sustainability of a token. Understanding how to effectively manage these two factors is essential for creating a successful token economy.

**Token Utility**

Token utility refers to the usefulness or functionality of a token within its ecosystem. The more practical applications a token has, the higher its utility value. Tokens can serve various functions such as access to a platform, payment for goods and services, governance rights, or even representing ownership of assets.

To enhance token utility, it is important to design a robust ecosystem that provides clear and tangible benefits for token holders. This can be achieved through partnerships with other projects, integration with popular platforms, or the development of innovative features that incentivize token usage.

Moreover, creating a strong demand for the token by offering exclusive benefits or discounts can also boost its utility value. By continuously improving and expanding the use cases of the token, the project can ensure its long-term viability and attractiveness to users.

**Token Scarcity**

Token scarcity refers to the limited supply of tokens available in the market. Scarcity is a fundamental economic principle that drives value by creating a sense of rarity and exclusivity. Tokens with a finite supply are more likely to appreciate in value over time, as increased demand meets limited availability.

To maintain token scarcity, it is essential to carefully manage the token distribution and supply dynamics. This can be achieved through mechanisms such as token burning, lock-up periods, or token buybacks. By reducing the circulating supply of tokens, the project can create artificial scarcity and drive up the token's value.

However, it is important to strike a balance between scarcity and accessibility. Overly restricting the token supply may hinder adoption and limit the token's utility, ultimately undermining its long-term value. Finding the right equilibrium between scarcity and usability is key to ensuring the sustainability of the token economy.

**Conclusion**

In conclusion, balancing token utility and scarcity is a complex but essential aspect of tokenomics. By maximizing token utility through practical applications and benefits, while maintaining a level of scarcity that drives value, projects can create a thriving and sustainable token economy. By carefully managing these two factors in tandem, token issuers can build a strong foundation for the success and longevity of their project.

**- Token velocity and its impact on the ecosystem**
Token velocity refers to the speed at which a token is circulated within a particular ecosystem. It is an important concept in tokenomics as it can have a significant impact on the overall health and stability of a token economy. In this section, we will explore the concept of token velocity and its implications for the ecosystem.

Token velocity is influenced by various factors, including the frequency of token transactions, the size of the token holder base, and the token's use cases within the ecosystem. A high token velocity indicates that tokens are changing hands quickly, while a low token velocity suggests that tokens are being held for longer periods.

High token velocity can have both positive and negative impacts on the ecosystem. On the positive side, a high token velocity can lead to increased liquidity and trading volume, which can enhance price discovery and market efficiency. It can also promote widespread adoption of the token and drive up demand, which can be beneficial for the token's value.

However, high token velocity can also have negative consequences. For example, frequent trading and rapid turnover of tokens can lead to increased price volatility, making it difficult for investors to predict price movements. High token velocity can also result in a lack of long-term holders, which may undermine the token's stability and hinder its utility as a store of value.

On the other hand, low token velocity implies that tokens are being held for longer periods, which can have its own set of implications. While low token velocity may contribute to price stability and reduce volatility, it can also limit liquidity and hinder the token's adoption and use within the ecosystem. Additionally, low token velocity may indicate a lack of interest or engagement with the token, which could impact its overall success.

In order to maintain a healthy token economy, it is important to strike a balance between high and low token velocity. Ecosystem designers and token issuers should consider the implications of token velocity on the ecosystem and implement strategies to manage and optimize it accordingly. This may involve incentivizing long-term holding, promoting token utility, and fostering a vibrant and active community of token holders.

Overall, token velocity is a key metric in tokenomics that can provide valuable insights into the dynamics of a token economy. By understanding the impact of token velocity on the ecosystem and implementing appropriate measures to address it, stakeholders can help ensure the long-term sustainability and success of the token economy.

## - Tools and methodologies for analyzing tokenomics models

Analyzing tokenomics models is crucial for understanding the underlying mechanisms of a digital asset and evaluating its potential for long-term success. There are several tools and methodologies that can be employed to effectively analyze tokenomics models. In this section, we will discuss some key approaches that can be used by researchers, investors, and blockchain enthusiasts to gain insights into the token economics of a project.

1. Tokenomics Frameworks: One of the fundamental tools for analyzing tokenomics models is the use of tokenomics frameworks. These frameworks provide a structured approach to evaluating various aspects of a token's economic design, such as token distribution, token utility, governance mechanisms, and incentives for various stakeholders. Examples of popular tokenomics frameworks include the Token Engineering Canvas, the Tokenomics Canvas, and the TEC Framework.

2. Token Metrics Analysis: Token metrics refer to quantitative data related to a token, such as supply, distribution, circulation, market capitalization, trading volume, and more. Analyzing token metrics can provide valuable insights into the economic dynamics of a token, including its market demand, liquidity, and potential for growth. Tools like CoinMarketCap, CoinGecko, and Token Metrics can be used to gather and analyze token metrics data.

3. Game Theory Analysis: Game theory is a powerful tool for analyzing the strategic interactions between different actors within a token ecosystem. By applying game theory principles, analysts can evaluate the incentives, behaviors, and outcomes of various stakeholders in the ecosystem, such as token holders, developers, miners, and users. Game theory models can help predict how participants will act under different scenarios and inform decision-making

processes.

4. Network Analysis: Network analysis involves studying the relationships and interactions between different entities within a token ecosystem. By mapping out the network structure and analyzing network dynamics, researchers can gain insights into how information, value, and influence flow through the system. Network analysis tools like GraphSense, Gephi, and NetworkX can be used to visualize and analyze token ecosystem networks.

5. Economic Modeling: Economic modeling involves creating mathematical models to simulate and analyze the economic behavior of a token ecosystem. By modeling factors such as token supply, demand, inflation, deflation, and user adoption, analysts can forecast the long-term sustainability and viability of a token project. Economic modeling tools like Monte Carlo simulations, agent-based modeling, and econometric models can be applied to study tokenomics dynamics.

6. Sentiment Analysis: Sentiment analysis involves tracking and analyzing public sentiment, opinions, and emotions related to a token project. By monitoring social media, forums, news outlets, and other sources, analysts can gauge the overall sentiment surrounding a token and identify potential market trends and risks. Sentiment analysis tools like Social Mention, Hootsuite, and Brandwatch can be used to track and analyze token sentiment.

In conclusion, analyzing tokenomics models requires a multidisciplinary approach that combines tools and methodologies from economics, game theory, network science, and data analytics. By leveraging these tools effectively, analysts can gain a deeper understanding of a token's economic design, assess its potential risks and rewards, and make informed decisions about investing or participating in a token ecosystem.

# Chapter 5: Token Valuation and Metrics

## - Valuation methods for tokens

Valuation methods for tokens are essential in the field of tokenomics, as they help investors and stakeholders understand the worth and potential of a token within a blockchain ecosystem. In this section, we will explore various valuation methods commonly used in tokenomics:

1. Market Capitalization (Market Cap): Market capitalization is one of the most straightforward valuation methods for tokens. It is calculated by multiplying the current price of a token by the total number of tokens in circulation. Market cap gives a rough estimate of a token's total value in the market and is often used as a benchmark for comparing different tokens.

2. Discounted Cash Flow (DCF) Analysis: DCF analysis is a fundamental valuation method used in traditional finance and can also be applied to tokens. This method involves estimating the future cash flows generated by a token project and discounting them back to their present value. DCF analysis helps in determining the intrinsic value of a token based on its potential future earnings.

3. Comparative Valuation: Comparative valuation involves comparing the token in question with similar tokens or projects in the market. This method considers factors such as the project's technology, team, market potential, and growth prospects to determine a fair value for the token. Comparative valuation can provide insights into how a token is positioned relative to its peers.

4. Token Utility Valuation: Token utility valuation focuses on assessing the value of a token based on its utility within the blockchain ecosystem. Factors such as the token's use cases, demand for the services it enables, and the overall adoption of the platform can influence its valuation. Tokens with high utility and strong network effects are likely to have higher valuations.

5. Network Value to Transactions (NVT) Ratio: The NVT ratio is a valuation metric that compares a token's market cap to the value of transactions conducted on its network. A low NVT ratio may indicate that the token is undervalued relative to the level of network activity, while a high ratio could signal overvaluation. The NVT ratio can provide insights into the efficiency and adoption of a token's network.

6. Token Velocity Analysis: Token velocity measures the rate at which a token is circulated within the ecosystem. A high token velocity may indicate that the token is being used frequently for transactions, while a low velocity could suggest hoarding or lack of demand. Token velocity analysis helps in understanding the dynamics of token circulation and its impact on valuation.

In conclusion, valuation methods for tokens play a crucial role in assessing the value and potential of blockchain projects. By utilizing a combination of quantitative and qualitative approaches, investors can make informed decisions about investing in tokens based on their intrinsic value, market dynamics, and utility within the ecosystem.

**- Key metrics to evaluate the health and performance of a token economy**

Evaluating the health and performance of a token economy is essential for investors, stakeholders, and developers to make informed decisions. There are several key metrics that can be used to assess the overall health and performance of a token economy. These metrics provide valuable insights into the network's growth, sustainability, and potential for long-term success. Below are some of the key metrics used to evaluate the health and performance of a token economy:

1. Market Capitalization: Market capitalization is a key metric used to assess the overall value and size of a token economy. It is calculated by multiplying the

current price of the token by the total number of tokens in circulation. A high market capitalization indicates a large and established token economy, while a low market capitalization may suggest limited adoption and potential risks.

2. Trading Volume: Trading volume measures the total amount of tokens traded on exchanges within a specific timeframe. High trading volume indicates a liquid market with active trading activity, while low trading volume may suggest limited interest or liquidity issues.

3. Token Velocity: Token velocity measures the rate at which tokens are being circulated within the ecosystem. A high token velocity indicates that tokens are being exchanged frequently, which can impact the token's value and stability. Understanding token velocity is important for assessing the token's utility and demand within the ecosystem.

4. Network Activity: Network activity measures the level of user engagement and activity within the token ecosystem. This can include metrics such as the number of active addresses, transactions per day, and unique token holders. High network activity indicates a vibrant and growing ecosystem, while low network activity may suggest stagnation or lack of interest.

5. Token Distribution: Token distribution refers to how tokens are allocated and held within the ecosystem. A well-distributed token economy is characterized by a diverse and decentralized ownership structure, which can help prevent centralization and manipulation. Evaluating token distribution can provide insights into the level of decentralization and security within the ecosystem.

6. Governance Participation: Governance participation measures the level of community involvement and decision-making within the token ecosystem. This can include metrics such as the number of votes cast, proposals submitted, and governance participation rate. Active governance participation is crucial for ensuring transparency, accountability, and consensus within the ecosystem.

7. Security and Resilience: Security and resilience metrics assess the network's ability to withstand external threats and attacks. This can include metrics such as the level of decentralization, security audits, and historical security incidents. Evaluating security and resilience can help identify potential vulnerabilities and risks that may impact the token economy's long-term viability.

By monitoring and analyzing these key metrics, stakeholders can gain valuable insights into the health and performance of a token economy. These metrics can help inform investment decisions, governance strategies, and ecosystem development efforts, ultimately contributing to the long-term success and sustainability of the token economy.

- Token price dynamics and factors influencing token value

Token price dynamics refer to the movement or fluctuations in the price of a token in a given market. Understanding the factors that influence token value is crucial for investors, token issuers, and other stakeholders in the cryptocurrency space. In this section, we will delve into the various factors that can impact the price of a token and contribute to its value.

1. Supply and Demand: The basic economic principle of supply and demand plays a significant role in determining the price of a token. If there is a high demand for a token but a limited supply, the price is likely to increase. Conversely, if the supply of a token outweighs the demand, the price may decrease.

2. Market Sentiment: Market sentiment, or the overall attitude of investors and traders towards a particular token, can have a major impact on its price. Positive news, partnerships, or developments related to a token can drive up its value, while negative news or regulatory actions can lead to a decline.

3. Utility and Use Case: The utility and use case of a token play a crucial role in determining its value. Tokens that have real-world applications, such as facilitating transactions, accessing services, or voting rights within a platform, are likely to have higher value than those with limited utility.

4. Tokenomics: The tokenomics of a project, including factors such as token distribution, token supply, and token burn mechanisms, can influence the price of a token. Projects with well-thought-out tokenomics models that incentivize holding and usage of the token are more likely to see price appreciation.

5. Market Capitalization: The market capitalization of a token, calculated by multiplying the current price by the total supply, is often used as a measure of a token's value. Tokens with higher market capitalization are generally perceived as more valuable and may attract more investors.

6. Competition and Innovation: The level of competition in the market and the degree of innovation offered by a token project can impact its price. Projects that stand out for their unique features, technology, or market positioning may command a higher value compared to competitors.

7. Regulatory Environment: Regulatory developments and changes can have a significant impact on the price of a token. Positive regulatory clarity and supportive frameworks can boost investor confidence and drive up token value, while regulatory uncertainty or restrictions may lead to a decrease in price.

8. Market Trends and External Factors: External factors such as macroeconomic trends, geopolitical events, and market sentiment towards cryptocurrencies as a whole can influence token prices. Being aware of these broader market dynamics is essential for understanding the price movements of tokens.

In conclusion, token price dynamics are influenced by a complex interplay of factors, ranging from basic economic principles to regulatory developments and market sentiment. By closely monitoring these factors and conducting thorough research, investors can make informed decisions regarding token investments based on an understanding of the underlying value drivers.

- Case studies of successful token projects and their valuation strategies

In the rapidly evolving world of blockchain and cryptocurrencies, there have been many successful token projects that have gained significant traction and adoption. These projects have implemented unique valuation strategies that have contributed to their success. In this section, we will explore some notable case studies of successful token projects and analyze the valuation strategies they have employed.

1. Ethereum (ETH): Ethereum is a decentralized platform that enables developers to build and deploy smart contracts and decentralized applications (dApps). The valuation strategy employed by Ethereum is based on the utility of its native token, Ether (ETH). Ether is used to pay for transaction fees and computational services on the Ethereum network, making it an essential component of the platform's ecosystem. The valuation of Ether is closely tied to the adoption and usage of the Ethereum network, as well as the demand for decentralized applications built on the platform.

2. Binance Coin (BNB): Binance Coin is the native token of the Binance cryptocurrency exchange, one of the largest and most popular exchanges in the world. BNB has a unique valuation strategy that revolves around its utility within the Binance ecosystem. Users can use BNB to pay for trading fees on the Binance platform, participate in token sales on Binance Launchpad, and access various other features and services. The demand for BNB is driven by the growth of the Binance exchange and the increasing number of users utilizing BNB for various purposes.

3. Uniswap (UNI): Uniswap is a decentralized exchange (DEX) built on the Ethereum blockchain that enables users to swap ERC-20 tokens without the need for an intermediary. The valuation strategy of Uniswap is closely linked to the governance and utility of its native token, UNI. UNI holders have voting rights to propose and vote on changes to the protocol, as well as access to liquidity mining rewards. The value of UNI is influenced by the growth of the Uniswap platform, the volume of trades conducted on the exchange, and the participation of the community in governance activities.

4. Chainlink (LINK): Chainlink is a decentralized oracle network that enables smart contracts to securely interact with external data sources. The valuation strategy of Chainlink is based on the demand for its services as a reliable and secure oracle solution. Chainlink's native token, LINK, is used to pay node operators for retrieving and delivering external data to smart contracts. The value of LINK is influenced by the adoption of Chainlink's oracle services by decentralized applications, blockchain platforms, and enterprises requiring external data integration.

In conclusion, successful token projects have implemented valuation strategies that align with the utility, adoption, and growth of their respective platforms and ecosystems. By focusing on providing real value, building strong communities, and continuously innovating, these projects have been able to achieve sustainable growth and success in the competitive cryptocurrency market.

# Chapter 6: Future Trends and Challenges in Tokenomics

## - Emerging trends in the field of tokenomics

As the field of tokenomics continues to evolve, several emerging trends are shaping the way tokens are used and valued within the blockchain ecosystem. These trends are indicative of the maturation and expansion of the token economy, offering new opportunities and challenges for businesses, investors, and consumers alike. In this section, we will explore some of the key emerging trends in the field of tokenomics:

1. Decentralized Finance (DeFi): One of the most significant trends in tokenomics is the rise of decentralized finance, or DeFi, which refers to the use of blockchain technology to recreate traditional financial systems in a decentralized manner. DeFi applications, such as decentralized exchanges, lending platforms, and automated market makers, are powered by tokens that enable users to participate in various financial activities without the need for intermediaries.

2. Non-Fungible Tokens (NFTs): NFTs have gained significant popularity in recent years, enabling the tokenization of unique digital assets such as art, collectibles, and virtual real estate. These tokens are non-interchangeable and represent ownership of a specific asset, providing new opportunities for creators and collectors to monetize and trade digital goods in a transparent and secure manner.

3. Tokenized Securities: Another emerging trend in tokenomics is the tokenization of traditional financial assets, such as stocks, bonds, and real estate. By converting these assets into tokens, issuers can streamline the process of issuing and trading securities, reduce costs, and increase liquidity for investors. Tokenized securities also offer new possibilities for fractional ownership and

global investment opportunities.

4. Governance Tokens: Governance tokens are tokens that grant holders the right to participate in the governance of a decentralized protocol or platform. Holders can vote on proposals, suggest changes, and influence the direction of the project, creating a more democratic and community-driven ecosystem. Governance tokens have become increasingly popular in decentralized organizations and blockchain networks.

5. Cross-Chain Compatibility: With the proliferation of blockchain networks and protocols, interoperability has become a key focus in the tokenomics space. Cross-chain compatibility enables tokens to be transferred and used across different blockchains, allowing for seamless integration and collaboration between disparate networks. Projects that prioritize cross-chain compatibility are well-positioned to tap into the full potential of the token economy.

6. Sustainability and Environmental Concerns: As the environmental impact of blockchain technology becomes more apparent, there is a growing emphasis on sustainability and energy efficiency in tokenomics. Projects that prioritize eco-friendly solutions, such as proof-of-stake consensus mechanisms or carbon offset programs, are gaining traction among environmentally conscious users and investors.

7. Regulatory Compliance: As the regulatory landscape around cryptocurrencies and tokens continues to evolve, projects are increasingly focused on ensuring compliance with relevant laws and regulations. Regulatory clarity and transparency are essential for the long-term viability of tokenized assets, and projects that proactively address compliance issues are more likely to gain trust and legitimacy in the market.

In conclusion, the field of tokenomics is experiencing rapid innovation and diversification, driven by emerging trends that are reshaping the way tokens are created, distributed, and utilized. By staying abreast of these trends and adapting to the evolving landscape, businesses and investors can navigate the complexities of the token economy and seize new opportunities for growth and innovation.

## - Challenges and limitations of existing tokenomics models

While tokenomics has gained significant popularity in the realm of blockchain and cryptocurrency, there are several challenges and limitations associated with existing tokenomics models. These challenges can impact the success and sustainability of token-based projects and should be carefully considered by developers, investors, and other stakeholders. Some of the key challenges and limitations include:

1. Lack of Regulation: One of the primary challenges facing tokenomics models is the lack of clear regulatory frameworks. The regulatory landscape surrounding tokens and cryptocurrencies is still evolving, leading to uncertainty and potential legal risks for token projects. Without clear guidelines and oversight, tokenomics models may struggle to gain mainstream acceptance and face regulatory backlash.

2. Volatility and Speculation: The inherent volatility of cryptocurrency markets poses a significant challenge to tokenomics models. Price fluctuations can impact the value of tokens and undermine the stability of token-based ecosystems. Additionally, speculative trading practices can distort token prices and hinder the organic growth of token economies.

3. Governance and Decision-Making: Tokenomics models often involve complex governance structures that rely on community participation and consensus mechanisms. However, coordinating decision-making processes among diverse stakeholders can be challenging, leading to conflicts, delays, and inefficiencies. Ensuring effective governance is crucial for the long-term sustainability of token projects.

4. Scalability and Interoperability: As blockchain technology continues to evolve, scalability and interoperability have emerged as key challenges for tokenomics models. Scalability limitations can hamper the growth of token economies, while interoperability issues can restrict the seamless exchange of tokens across different platforms and networks. Overcoming these technical challenges is essential for the widespread adoption of tokenomics models.

5. Security and Privacy Concerns: Tokenomics models rely on blockchain technology, which is not immune to security vulnerabilities and privacy risks. Smart contract bugs, hacking attacks, and data breaches can undermine the integrity of token-based systems and erode user trust. Addressing security and privacy concerns is crucial for safeguarding the assets and information stored within token economies.

6. Token Distribution and Fairness: The initial distribution of tokens plays a significant role in shaping the dynamics of tokenomics models. Unequal token distribution, concentration of wealth, and lack of transparency in token issuance can lead to centralization and inequality within token ecosystems. Ensuring fair and inclusive token distribution mechanisms is essential for fostering a vibrant and sustainable token economy.

In conclusion, while tokenomics holds great promise for revolutionizing various industries, it is essential to acknowledge and address the challenges and limitations that can impede the success of token-based projects. By carefully considering these factors and implementing robust strategies to overcome them, stakeholders can navigate the complexities of tokenomics and harness its transformative potential.

- **Potential regulatory developments and their implications on token economies**

As the blockchain and cryptocurrency industry continues to evolve, regulatory developments play a crucial role in shaping the landscape of token economies. It is essential for participants in the tokenomics space to stay informed about potential regulatory changes and understand how they might impact their projects and investments. In this section, we will explore some of the potential regulatory developments and their implications on token economies.

1. Regulatory Clarity: One of the primary challenges in the tokenomics space has been the lack of regulatory clarity. Many jurisdictions are still in the process of defining how tokens should be regulated, whether they are considered securities, commodities, or something else entirely. As regulators around the world continue to grapple with these questions, clear guidelines and regulations are expected to emerge. This regulatory clarity will provide more certainty to token projects and investors, potentially boosting confidence in the market.

2. Compliance Requirements: With increased regulatory scrutiny, token projects will likely face stricter compliance requirements. This could include mandatory KYC (Know Your Customer) and AML (Anti-Money Laundering) procedures, as well as adherence to securities laws. Token issuers will need to ensure that their projects are compliant with relevant regulations, which could increase operational costs and administrative burden. However, compliance with regulations can also enhance trust and legitimacy in the eyes of investors and regulators.

3. Licensing and Registration: Some jurisdictions may require token issuers, exchanges, and other participants in the token economy to obtain licenses or register with regulatory authorities. This can add an additional layer of oversight

and accountability to the industry, helping to weed out bad actors and fraudulent projects. However, the process of obtaining licenses can be time-consuming and costly, particularly for smaller token projects.

4. Taxation: Taxation is another area where regulatory developments could have a significant impact on token economies. Different jurisdictions have varying tax laws when it comes to cryptocurrencies and tokens, including how they are treated for income tax, capital gains tax, and other purposes. Token projects and investors will need to stay informed about tax regulations in their jurisdictions to ensure compliance and avoid potential penalties.

5. Market Stability: Regulatory developments can also influence market stability in the token economy. Well-designed regulations that provide clarity and protect investors can help to reduce volatility and promote a healthier market environment. On the other hand, overly restrictive or ambiguous regulations could stifle innovation and drive legitimate projects underground, potentially leading to market uncertainty and price fluctuations.

In conclusion, regulatory developments have the power to shape the future of token economies in significant ways. While increased regulation can bring stability and legitimacy to the industry, it also poses challenges for token projects and investors. By staying informed about potential regulatory changes and adapting to comply with evolving regulations, participants in the tokenomics space can navigate these challenges and contribute to a more robust and sustainable ecosystem.

**- Predictions for the future of tokenomics and its role in the broader financial ecosystem**

As we look towards the future of tokenomics, it is clear that this innovative field will continue to play a significant role in shaping the broader financial ecosystem.

The intersection of blockchain technology, cryptocurrencies, and tokenization has already begun to revolutionize traditional financial systems, and there are several key trends and predictions that can help us anticipate what the future holds for tokenomics.

1. Increased adoption of tokenized assets: One of the most notable predictions for the future of tokenomics is the increased adoption of tokenized assets across various industries. Tokenization allows for the fractional ownership of assets, which can unlock liquidity and lower barriers to entry for investors. We can expect to see a wide range of assets – such as real estate, art, stocks, and even intellectual property – being tokenized to create new investment opportunities and streamline asset management processes.

2. Mainstream integration of decentralized finance (DeFi): Decentralized finance, or DeFi, has gained significant traction in recent years by providing decentralized alternatives to traditional financial services such as lending, borrowing, and trading. In the future, we can anticipate the mainstream integration of DeFi protocols and platforms into the broader financial ecosystem, offering users more efficient, transparent, and accessible financial services.

3. Evolution of tokenomics models: As the tokenomics space continues to evolve, we can expect to see the development of new tokenomics models that better suit the needs of different projects and communities. This may include innovative token distribution mechanisms, governance structures, and incentive schemes that aim to enhance token utility and value creation.

4. Regulatory developments and compliance standards: With the growing popularity of cryptocurrencies and tokenized assets, regulators around the world are increasingly focusing on developing clear regulatory frameworks to govern these new financial instruments. In the future, we can expect to see more robust regulatory developments and compliance standards that aim to protect investors, prevent fraud, and ensure the legitimacy of tokenized projects.

5. Interoperability and cross-chain solutions: As the blockchain ecosystem continues to expand with multiple blockchains and token standards, interoperability and cross-chain solutions will become crucial for enabling seamless asset transfers and interactions between different blockchain networks. The development of interoperability protocols and standards will play a key role in fostering collaboration and innovation within the tokenomics space.

In conclusion, the future of tokenomics holds great promise for transforming the financial landscape by unlocking new opportunities, improving efficiency, and promoting financial inclusion. By staying abreast of these predictions and trends, stakeholders in the tokenomics space can better prepare for the exciting developments that lie ahead.

www.ingramcontent.com/pod-product-compliance
Lightning Source LLC
Chambersburg PA
CBHW070949220526
45471CB00007B/2952